BULLROARER

Other volumes in the series:

The Morse Poetry Prize
Edited by Guy Rotella

TED GENOWAYS

Bullroarer
A Sequence

THE 2001 MORSE
POETRY PRIZE
SELECTED AND
INTRODUCED BY
MARILYN HACKER

Northeastern University Press
BOSTON

Northeastern University Press

Library of Congress Cataloging-in-Publication Data
Genoways, Ted.
    Bullroarer : a sequence / Ted Genoways.
        p. cm. — (The 2001 Morse Poetry Prize)
    ISBN 1-55553-507-0 (acid-free paper)
    I. Title. II. Morse Poetry Prize ; 2001.
PS3557 .E435 B8 2001
811'.54—dc21

                                        2001037024

Designed by Ann Twombly

Composed in Weiss by Graphic Composition, Inc., Athens, Georgia. Printed and bound by Thomson-Shore, Inc., Dexter, Michigan. The paper is Writer's Offset, an acid-free stock.

MANUFACTURED IN THE UNITED STATES OF AMERICA
04   03   02   01   5   4   3   2   1

for my family and for Mary Anne

ACKNOWLEDGMENTS

Grateful acknowledgment is made to the journals where the follow-
ing poems appeared, many in earlier versions:

DoubleTake:	"8:15"
Midwest Quarterly:	"Pietà"
New England Review:	"Blaze"
New Republic:	"Outside the Slaughterhouse"
North Dakota Quarterly:	"For My Father, Who Does Not Dance"
Ploughshares:	Sections I, II, and IV of "The Bolt-struck Oak"
Prairie Schooner:	"The One Day"
Press:	"Uncle Earl and the War to End All Wars"
Quarterly West:	"Night Train," Section III of "The Bolt-struck Oak" (as "Depth of Field")
Shenandoah:	"Into the Storm"
Southern Poetry Review:	"The Cow Caught in the Ice," "The Dead Have a Way of Returning," "The Killing Floor"
Virginia Quarterly Review:	"Under the Big Top"
Witness:	"Bullroarer"

"The Cow Caught in the Ice" received the Guy Owen Poetry Prize
from *Southern Poetry Review* for 1997, selected by Jane Hirshfield.

"The Killing Floor" received the Guy Owen Poetry Prize from
Southern Poetry Review for 1998, selected by Walt McDonald.

"Pietà" was reprinted in *Anthology of Magazine Verse and Yearbook of
American Poetry 1995–1996* (Monitor Books, 1997).

"Like This, Slaughtering the Winter Sow" and "The Bolt-struck
Oak" received the 1998 Academy of American Poets Prize from the
University of Virginia.

A number of these poems also appeared in the chapbooks *The Dead Have a Way of Returning* (Brooding Heron Press, 1997) and *The Cow Caught in the Ice* (Soundpost Press, 1999).

"The Dead Have a Way of Returning" was issued as a limited edition broadside by The Press of Appletree Alley, 1994.

I would also like to thank my teachers, William Kloefkorn, Ted Kooser, Walt McDonald, William Wenthe, Charles Wright, Gregory Orr, and Rita Dove, for their careful reading and insightful comments on these poems, as well as my fellow members of the waitstaff and social staff at Bread Loaf. Special thanks to Lisa Russ Spaar, for her stalwart support, and to Robert Baker, for the hours spent on his ranch. My deepest gratitude to John McNally, Amy Knox Brown, and Cécile and Stewart Tucker for their years of friendship.

Contents

III

IV

Introduction

In a language of visceral accuracy made concise and more memorable by metric structure, Ted Genoways tells an American story that is also emblematic of a piece of American history—a history of expansion cruelly compressed by the Depression, a history of the movement from rural to urban and suburban life, from the collective autonomy of the family farm to the depersonalization of hired labor. This history is incarnated in that of one Nebraska farm family, then of one man, its youngest son, who was in fact the poet's eponymous grandfather. Genoways places himself in this first book in the line of a multiethnic group of contemporary poets writing in English who have used the generations of a family as a focus from which broader historical reflection is generated; some others are Seamus Heaney, Derek Walcott, Marilyn Nelson, Tony Harrison, Eavan Boland, Rita Dove—and, in the newer generation, Yvette Christiansë (who is South African) and Reetika Vazirani (from India), both now living in the United States. Is this a development that synthesizes the sixties emphasis on individual experience, inaccurately called "confessional" because it added the specific details of a lived life to the Romantic focus on a universalized "self," with the narrative and political thrust of Victorian poets like both Brownings and George Meredith? Or (and as well) does this welcome enlargement of viewpoint, in the case of Ted Genoways in particular, signal a recognition even on the part of white American poets (meaning *"étatsuniens"* here) that their experience is by no means universal, is as specific and as unique as any other, and that it merits a poetry that honors and evokes its singularity?

Perhaps it says something about the movement of American poetry that the stockyards and slaughterhouses choired in operatic open form by Carl Sandburg are rendered (a word that takes on another meaning in one poem) by Ted Genoways in a metered verse that spares the reader no detail. There is no romance to the blood and heat and animal terror communicated to workers (and readers) as it emanates from the killing floors of the Omaha meatpacking industry. Nor is there any prelapsarian idyll envisioned in the earlier day-by-day life of a family farm in the twentieth century's first years. This is, first and foremost, a book about work—in which it is central to the lives of men and women, in which perhaps the greatest human fulfillment is that of doing work one loves, whether it is the grandfather's building all the shelves and furniture in a house he finally owned but could not afford to furnish "store-bought," or the two-generations-distant-cousin's painting landscapes she had never seen from instructions in a correspondence course but finding satisfaction in the act of painting itself. Though much of the work this poet depicts is endured, not loved, it is "work" that opens the elegy at the close of the book.

> I can picture him only in the climate of work:
> letting a head of water through floodgates or
> stacking hay, silent and smooth as the baler's belt.
>
> For years on factory floors, he shoveled beet sugar
> into brown-paper bags. . . .
> ("Late Refrains for a Grandfather")

While contemporary American poetry has become almost obsessional in its focus on the family (the poet's family, usually "dysfunctional," seems to have replaced the erotic, tutelary, or numinous encounter center stage), the family is often seen as an isolated, almost asocial unit—or disunity. Genoways' turn-of-the-last-century farm family is a unit like a mountain-climbing expedition or a team of firefighters for whom cooperation is necessary for success and indeed for survival. The trope of the book's first section is the attempt to save lives—sometimes successfully, sometimes not.

Of course, the history of the forms the poet chooses inflects his narrative. Terza rima, Dante's meter for the *Commedia*, here becomes

the vehicle for a not-at-all metaphysical descent into the worst of
what human beings do as matter of fact: assembly-line slaughter. We
first experience the poet's terza rima in the Purgatory of the farm in
the book's opening sequences. Here there is work of all sorts: sowing
and planting, logging, building, herding, slaughtering and cooking,
and the work, too, of what we call "labor":

> The midwife says, *bite this strop*. Outside, burn-killed limbs—
> once wide as the province of God—lie piled in cords,
> sorted from kindling to cook logs. Lynn tears muslin
>
> into even strips, watching Wallace through the door
> drag the jagtooth back and forth.
> ("The Bolt-struck Oak")

The laboring mother, the midwife, the father and son cutting kin-
dling: a plethora of workers.
    Here there is senseless death as well (of newborn infants from
jaundice, of a cow separated from the herd and caught in the ice, in
a thunderstorm striking a circus tent at a fairground) and no easy
temporal resolution or epiphanic redemption. But this is not the
book's Inferno of the stockyards, the work-world of willed destruc-
tion of the slaughterhouses in which the elder Genoways, then a
young man of twenty-five, and his brother participate for survival in
1932. The image of cattle cars packed with victims on their way to
slaughter is, of course, not devoid of other resonances:

> His frosted eyes jitter from the boardinghouse roof
> to the tracks below, where a low-riding stake truck
> brakes by a frozen calf. Ted squints, his stare fixed
>
> on the workman, untying the tarp of his rig.
> When he peels the canvas back, Johannsen elbows
> Cullen and says, *Look-it*: dead cows piled three-high, legs
>
> grey and stiff as tipped sawhorses.
> ("The Killing Floor")

These five poems, and their pendant coda in that most unexpected and musical of forms, the villanelle, are the fiery depths of the book, to which its protagonist and its reader alike must descend, and then emerge in the light and lightness of the lines incorporating the refrain (after a bludgeoned steer brings down a man) of the youth's escape ("work" the key word once again).

> Steam twisting from the half-lit
> rails. Sheets drawn, footlocker missing,
> and he hasn't shown for work yet.
>   ("8:15")

    Bullroarer fulfills one essential test for a book of poems: not only does it merit rereading, but, after one has read the whole, the poems of each section become fuller, clearer, and more resonant with each return. I would have been moved and intrigued to discover any of these poems on its own, but the collection coheres into a powerful, memorable, and singular whole.

MARILYN HACKER

Each time I pass
by the cemetery,
I am drawn back by the power
that still blows through your bones.
　　　　—Miguel Hernández

Outside the Slaughterhouse

Some nights, following the interstate home,
I pull off at the stockyards to hear the drone
of butchering. The floodlight casts shadows
across the catwalk and the feedlot below.
Calves look up from their pens, eyes like polished
stones. In the distance, the Missouri twists
in its bed. This is where my grandfather,
sleepless nights, walked the banks; where water
turned red by sundown. Here, he scooped slit guts,
sawed bones. Here, the river's dull force still cuts.
The moon's crescent curves like a gambrel hook.
Clouds stall like freighted cattle cars. I stoop
to fill my pockets with rocks, cold and worn.
These too were mountains before I was born.

BULLROARER

"All tribes west of the Mississippi knew these ancient noisemakers . . . as the moaning of the wind that brings the thunderstorm and produces rain; only wood from a tree struck by lightning is acceptable for these sacred lightning sticks."

—Bernard Mason
The Book of Indian-Crafts and Costumes (1946)

I

The Cow Caught in the Ice

I. PREMONITION
Catherine Genoways, October 27, 1906

The last holstein sways to the mud hole, creamed with ice.
Owls drop from their roosts, clacking beaks against dusk, welled
without warning into barn eaves. The herd dog eyes

a shrew, chewing sap, then yelps and buries his tail.
The shrew moves deeper into cordwood. Cornstalks
sink into fields. Like corrugated tin, furrows

rill toward shelterbelts. Spruce sag with the weight of hawks,
their eyes lit by each burst before thunderclap. The bur-oak,
laid open by lightning, whose scorched branch caps still hold

split shells of spring hatch, whose roots now rise like lost bones,
slumps to the north. There: above treetops, the blue anvil,
below, the man, slapping herefords, drowned by groans,

their grey breath spiriting away. Across dark fields
his wife, bolting windows closed, receives her vision:
pens filled with ghosts of calves, years since gone to slaughter,

loose jaws churning black cud, eyes dull and unwishing,
their mothers' udders swing with mud and green water,
the children crouch, mouthing biscuits without butter—

II. PICKING DOWN THE ROWS
Lewis Cass Genoways, October 28

He tugs the broad-brim over his brow and whistles.
The bay's ears twitch. He spits, then spurs her toward the ridge,
where thistles poke through drifts, faded grey and brittle.

He pauses at the crest: to the west Chapman Bridge,
east the Burlington tracks—snake of smoke and boxcars,
coal-dark, shadowing valleys like a contour ditch.

On either side wire fences hum like strummed guitars.
He can almost remember a time when all this
was a blowing wilderness of grass, when the hiss

of wind whipped through bluestem like a cloudburst. He fears
her dead, that snow drifted in her nostrils, or ice
sealed her lips. When he calls over hills, all he hears

is a hoarse voice repeating, more sluggish each time,
less his own. When he was younger, he picked down rows
of apples, red as plums among leaves. One sundown,

a girl came from Pawnee camp, carrying armloads
of wheat chaff to trade as cattle feed. His boss frowned
and shook his head. He hears their laughter even now,

the girl turning home. Perhaps it was applejack
they sipped from steel cups that hoisted him to his feet.
He snaps the reins, the bay limping through snow dunes, back

to the barn. He brushes the horses down, drapes each
in wool blankets. He'll find her at sunup, sunken
to the withers, her eyes blue cataracts, tongue stiff.

In the remote orchards of Cedar Bluff, young, drunk,
and perfecting his curve with a jonathon smith,
that Pawnee girl might still swap winesap for a kiss.

Catherine, October 28

She watches for him by the window's leaded glass.
It ripples like tideline debris ringing edges
of summer ponds. As a girl, she crawled through tallgrass,

squeezing pollywogs till they shed their tails. Her ledges
hold vinegar and dillspice while she cooks, but nights
she lowers each jar till a circle forms around

the old Franklin stove. L.C. feeds a split rail-tie,
scavenged from the switchyard, into its grated mouth.
She rises first, her children still tucked in the loft,

and steps softly, now lifting each cold jar to rest
around the skillet. This is the time she covets:
when the stove is cool enough to touch, each hand pressed

hard against its belly to feel inside what's left
and almost breathing. The last four children drowned
in their beds before the pastor could hold their heads

under. *Jaundice,* doctor said, their stomachs so round
they were ready to pop. She can't live for the dead;
seven live mouths hang open. She slips back to bed—

two minutes till the coffee boils—but keeps one eye
on that orange egg purling across the frozen pane,
like watching her dad light stars in the nighttime sky,

making constellations of sheep pens, against rain
and wolves and the darkness that never died in years
after he did. *Go on sun, get up, sweeten snow*

into warm rivers. It's all of those things she fears:
glass is fire and sand, water expands in the cold.
Seconds now, hold your breath—the kettle's lips explode.

IV. ANNUNCIATION
Catherine and Lewis Cass, October 29

When he finds her, he tromps to the barn, bridles
and harnesses the horse. He drops a ballpeen and chain
in a leather satchel, tucks his widest chisel

under his arm. Meat, by now, crystals on the bone.
He carves a circle and wrestles the last milk cow
to shore. It's near dusk. He boots her purpled udder

and the bag splits like a single-stitch seam but no
blood, no milk. He locks the front gate while dogs turn
circles at his feet. Tonight, he will let them burn

beside the stove, twitching through thickets, thumping tails.
His wife cooks and watches out windows shuttered tight.
He sits. He eats. One by one, children become bales

for him to hoist up the ladder. *If the horse died*
that would have been worse. Or any of these children.
He piles on crazy quilts sewn from his worn-out shirts.

He snuffs the lamplight, whispers, *I'm sorry, Catherine,*
into the sagging moons of her breasts, her weak heart
drumming so hard he wonders if her ribs might split.

Outside, the wind picks up again, hard flakes ticking
at the window, wheeling upward, swirling around
empty limbs of the cottonwood and hickory,

drifting, eddying over the blue-rigid cow,
filling the dark circle of water her body
left round and wanting. Tomorrow, four Pawnee men

will dig out the drift and cut the cold-burned body
into pieces to feed families of bone and skin.
He covers her mouth, so she won't stir the children.

Like This, Slaughtering the Winter Sow

Lewis Cass and Wallace Genoways, December 6, 1906

He squeezes the blue heart like this in his glove
until clots break and spill on his feet.
Dad doesn't couple this muscle with love.

He says, *Feel the thrum. You have to be rough.*
To show me, he murmurs *da-dum* for each beat
and squeezes the blue heart like this in his glove.

He carves and curses the sow for being tough,
her thighs turned rope by heavy teats.
Dad doesn't couple her muscle with love.

He grinds scraps with black pepper and clove,
stuffs her feet in vinegar jars. Nearly complete,
he squeezes the blue heart—*like this*—in his glove,

like this, he says, *like wringing a sponge.*
I close my fist, refuse to touch the meat.
Dad doesn't couple this muscle with love;

he's fleeing a vision: his wife like a potbelly stove.
Like this—his arms bulge—*or mama won't eat,*
and he squeezes the blue heart like this in his glove.
Dad doesn't couple this muscle with love.

The Bolt-struck Oak

For they have sown the wind and shall reap the whirlwind.
                                              —Hosea 8:7

I. LABOR
  Theodore Thompson Genoways, born June 24, 1907

The midwife says, *bite this strop.* Outside, burn-killed limbs—
once wide as the province of God—lie piled in cords,
sorted from kindling to cook logs. Lynn tears muslin

into even strips, watching Wallace through the door
drag the jagtooth back and forth. His father totters
the branch until it breaks free in his hand, then points

to the next. The girls drop pails—half-filled with water,
half with silt—swelling dust from under the floor joists.
They pour into a cookpot, now nearing a boil.

Wallace buckles the saw to free it from binding,
but three tines snap. He feels the break, gap-toothed and wet
with sap, then turns to his father, stacking behind him,

and calls, *should we save out in case of a casket?*
The midwife wipes her glasses, grips the baby's crown,
whispers, *now when I tell you, I want you to bite,*

then twists, so the shoulders slip past. When he cries out,
she cuts the cord. His father—in the day's last light—
bends Wallace to the stump, belt arcing like a scythe.

8

II. DROUGHT
Lewis Cass and Catherine Genoways, August 4, 1907

L.C. wonders if it ever rains where she is.
Though he could straighten his arm across the mattress
to touch her side, he knows—like oceans of cheatgrass

choking snakeweed and sage—the sick baby constricts
her roots. Parts of her brittle like winter-killed corn.
The day he chained the team to the dead oak and pulled,

something buried bent, then cracked. The baby was born,
and rootstock snapped like bones till the rough trunk jolted
the ground. At the glass all night, she stared at the hole,

while he lay in his cradle, silent and yellow.
He still never cries, and the doctor says sun's
the best cure, as if there were somewhere she could go

for shade. She twirls the sawtooth leaf between her thumb
and finger, wishing for the wind's slow whisper back
like mist on the roof. L.C.'s in the barn, truing

planks for a floor. From where she sits, he ebbs in black.
She can't see rills of sweat or him stretch, then loosen
his shirt, or hear—high in the rafters—doves cooing

between thrusts of the plane. He inches a level
down the board's length, squinting. He doesn't see her breasts
pale against the jaundiced child. He squares by bevel,

preferring straight lines to her curves where the boy rests
and suckles. Tonight she undresses by lamplight
and slips into bed. L.C. curls her like a spoon,

murmuring how oak retains the quiet of night
well past dawn, but she dreams of hills thick with fescue.
Curtains draw open, cut clover fills every room.

III. DEPTH OF FIELD
Theodore and Goldie Louise Genoways, August 8, 1907

Goldie holds her arms out, stiff as a drying-horse,
and her mother places the baby in her lap,
folding Goldie's wrists, then lacing her white fingers

till they cradle the bowl of his middle, fat
as the bulb of an oil-lamp. The photographer
cranes his neck—the kitchen dim, but dense with noon heat,

sun beating on tin planks nailed to the bare rafters—
then twists the aperture. Goldie shifts in her seat
and Ted cries. Still, the man steadies a metal sheet

in his palm and sprinkles magnesium powder,
so she begins—after his drape falls and wick tips,
but before smoke billows, before even the flare

or pop, his words *don't blink* yet on the air—begins
to sing a lullaby, so that when they emerge
from the printer's fix, her lips are slightly open,

and what she finds is not herself, or her brother,
or the kitchen, but what the unblinking discern:
their farm cast in the brown grain of sepia tone—

their oak table turned butternut in the cream-glow,
flowing from the window to the open cupboard,
faced with false willowware, its blues washed to yellow

and rust. Behind them the dead ground, endless scrub-board
of empty furrows, and—where the bur-oak once rose—
a dirt mound like a fresh grave. But at this storm's core,

Goldie's flaxen hair, a single blonde cowlick, floats
over her sallow brother, cradled in her arms.
Fallowed fields, her father says, *yield twice the sweetcorn.*

IV. FLUX: THE TURNING
Lewis Cass, August 29, 1907

The baby—bloated with bile—attracts chicken hawks.
The doctor says flux is normal, just his liver
unsouring. Still, they twist thick as flies. Dusk: cur dogs

crouch where the windbreak slopes south toward the river.
As a boy, L.C. watched a pack close on a calf—
sick from still water—licking the green from its tail.

He prowls the fenceline, following the shotgun's shaft
like a snout. One coyote snapped the calf's flank. It wailed
like a newborn and buckled. He stiffens, then wheels

back toward the house. Light leaks from each windowpane,
sending lattice shadows across the grass, stunted
and sunwashed grey. In the distance, a cattle train

sounds its whistle, and one of the dogs cocks its head.
He levels and fires—a flare like lightning bursting
in a pair of ember eyes. The calf tried to bawl

but coyotes tore the tongue from its mouth, blood coursing
in streaming ropes. Sunup, he'll find the half-breed balled
in a bed of indian grass, clotted and smaller

than he hoped. He grips it by the scruff. Catherine
on the grass beats dust from the rugs, while the three girls
dandle their brother. In a stand of big bluestem,

he stacks branches around the carcass, cuts and piles
underbrush, then tramps to the house, grey thunderhead
climbing the ridge. He shoves the wellcap to the ground.

First drops—dimpling the dirt—redden and spread
like blossoms or blood. He calls Wallace from the house,
and they ride out together to herd in the cows.

Landscape with Crows

Among the rat's nests of rags and glass insulators,
    scattered on the worn planks of the attic floor,

a stack of oil paintings lay wrapped in canvas.
    We drove all morning to get to that house

where my mother spent her summers as a girl.
    But now that we were there, hunched below the rafters,

listening to the windows flute and trill, it was not
    the familiar images of hayrakes and rusted trucks

or meadow grass whipping back and forth across
    empty fields that she wanted, but these still lifes

and pastorals of far-off places. In the silence
    of her upstairs room, my mother's cousin Alice

followed the words of the correspondence packet
    in every detail, stirred her palette to make colors

she had never seen. Her peaches and raspberries
    looked warm and soft-lit. A fireglow yellowed

the window of the little country cottage set
    among the evergreens as the horse-drawn sleigh

approached through the snow. What she wanted most
    was the cool of the canvas, just before

the brush interrupts its calm, like a summer pond
    with a rower stroking so slowly that no ripples

move out from the bow and the black surface reflects
    nothing. Out there, in the cricket-thick heat

of those summer nights, my mother would slip
    to the bunkhouse where her father

and the other hired men had to sleep. Weary from
   stooping under the hoods of farm trucks

or greasing the feed-grinder shaft, he would kiss
   her forehead, then fall back to snoring.

Moonlight turned the lampblack sky a deep
   cobalt blue and the wind of forty years sand-pocked

the abandoned farmhouse to flake-white. That morning
   as we lowered the paintings through the attic door

and carried them, still wrapped in the flapping canvas,
   to our station wagon, the sun-blear burned

in my memory those twin sienna tracks that snaked
   through fields of ochre and indian yellow.

If I remember my mother's stories of how her dad
   chopped the heads from rattlers with a hoe

or picture rows of tipped stones for snakebitten children
   in the Bodarc Cemetery, it's only because it seemed

as foreign and wonderful to me then as the cliffs
   of France must have seemed to Alice. Alone

in her tiny corner room, she scraped her knife
   across the bare plain of her palette and dreamed

that one day she would see more than earth and sky,
   one day just drive and never come home. She heard

the tractor roar and hum. From the stillness of her easel
   she turned back to the chaos of the world, framed

for a moment by her windowpane: the slow mower
   adrift on fields of hay, the sky alive with crows.

II

Pietà

What we remember
are not hours, or days,
but moments
come as ghosts, slim as darkness
itself.
            Night is like that, ghosts
all around, the rain, the wind,
the flashlight darting into places
we shouldn't see until morning.
The cottonwood has fallen,
we're in the rain, the lodgepole pine leans
over,
            and you, my mother,
momentarily under the lightning,
caress the white pine, lifted wholly
from its roots, grieving as only mother
can her child, *Beautiful, so beautiful.*

Uncle Earl and the War to End All Wars

November 11, 1995

Uncle Earl plowed his fields
at night after rain, when the tractor's light
might glint off a bit of brass or flint
like a star surrendered to the dirt.

He sifted clods through his fingers,
humming those songs he carried
like bits of wars he hadn't fought.
I never asked about the one he did

after his story: the first lesson
the DI taught was *hold on to your rifle.*
But keep the lids from K rations
in case—more than one man's life saved

by fisting the enemy's hair
and slitting his throat with the tin.
Uncle Earl knew a man trapped in Berlin
who killed four soldiers with a shovel

before finding one finally with a rifle.
Germans were out there, ready to kill
for wood and steel. He clutched the barrel
until the skin on his knuckles split.

Every bomb bloomed closer.
Sometimes he thought they hunted
him. So he shook arrowheads
and buttons in his pockets, sang hymns.

I want to tell all this to red-faced boys
whooping at dogfighters buzzing
the stadium before the holiday game,
to say that rum smuggled in their Cokes

is all the painkiller they get,
snarl at the one gnashing a hot dog
what *smothered in mustard*
once meant. When he elbows his buddy

and crows, *They were afraid of that thing?*
I want to bandage his head
like a shell-shock victim and lead him
to the ranch in Temple, Aunt Rhea waiting

at the screendoor. Say this was your wife
and screaming kids. Live long enough
for one stupid nephew to show you
his plastic jeep and ask if you want

to fight. Uncle Earl turned a toy like that
in his hands, clouds forming on his brow
seeing steel axles. He said, *Boy,
do you know what this metal's worth?*

No one did, until the clouds burst
into lightning that night in August.
In pajamas, he grabbed his shovel
and gun, ran to a trenched creek bed,

and dug. He bellied down in that foxhole
till the storm washed gullies
and he rolled and began to float.
The doctor blamed his heart, stopped

by water and cold. Uncle Earl waited years
for rain like that, his nights
already split by spitfire and clouds,
where every showered blessing is a bomb.

Under the Big Top

near Grand Island, Nebraska, July 23, 1913

I.

Fields of flax and sweetcorn flash under a half-moon
climbing the trellised treeline. Distant clouds tremble
each time the horizon flares and the mare's hipbones

glisten as if sunlit. She snorts, shakes her bridle,
but Ted's mother tightens the reins, cooing what seems
almost a love song over the throb of their wheels

against wagon ruts, grass swishing the axletree.
He shuts his eyes and listens: peepers, cicadas,
wind in the cottonwoods. When he rouses from sleep,

they're nearing the fairgrounds. Kerosene bulbs, abuzz
with june bugs, swing from the tent poles. A light drizzle
has begun to fall, and Ted watches the shadows of boys

sway toward the big top, lamps bobbing like thistles.
A nighthawk calls, faint as a distant train whistle.

11.

L.C. lets the door slap, lifts the whistling kettle
from the stove with a dishtowel. Granary patched
with tinscrap, cobs ground and slopped for the cattle,

evening has crept in like the dull ache in his back.
He blows steam from his cup, watching out the window.
Soon his boys will come following the footpath

over the ridge. Single file and nodding like cows,
they will drop their tools, jog to the night-cooled river,
and shed their sweat-crusted clothes, strung from the willows,

till the moon is high overhead. The four others
jaundiced in their cribs, before they even had names.
Mostly what he remembers is the scent of cedar,

clawhammer, sixpenny nails, the chuck of the plane.
He remembers the rattling cart, digging their graves.

III.

Sunset. Knee-deep in corn. Wallace driving the spade.
Down the row, Lynn in silhouette squats to knock dirt
from the lacy roots of cocklebur and bindweed,

then stands, wiping his hands on the tail of his shirt,
its thin denim touched with the deep rust of dusk
and clay. But all is bleached white by the time they work

the last groove, stooped under a half-moon, amid husks
rustling, dark trees rocking at the top of the ridge.
In the distance, the night train kicks clouds of white dust

into the air, rumbles over the wood-frame bridge,
so the moon shivers on the face of the river.
Now, his spade still, the whistle sounds like a pigeon

roosted high in the rafters of the old house; firs
rise like bedposts into a canopy of stars.

IV.

Under the canopy—snapping like a tattered flag—
the wirewalker shoulders her balance. It wobbles,
sagged at each end, but her feet creep down the rope rigged

between the tallest poles. The tent walls mottle
with lamplight and shadow, dumb show of elephants,
tumbling clowns, spinning like sun through a milk bottle.

Goldie steals a glimpse of the others. Eyes round
with fear, their stares are fixed on a woman, standing
arms wide on a swaybacked, sequin-studded stallion,

but then the horse stops, midair, its rider dangling
like the wirewalker between sky and earth: the hiss
and sizzle of the struck post, the thunderclap, screaming

and sawdust, people running for the flame-lit tracks
where caged animals howl at the edge of darkness.

V.

Storm gales howl in the darkness, whipping treetops side
to side. Rain streams from Bob's hat brim. Huddled here
at the far edge of the woods, his unsteady steed

stamping the underbrush into black mud, he stares
across the acreage, where corn rows sink in the glut.
Last spring, he aimed the drafthorse like a rifle—ears

solid as a sight—at the pine grove across the Platte.
Without bit or blinders, he cut each furrow, straight
as new corduroy. Now hailstones beat green stalks flat.

Ditchwater swells and gushes over the floodgate.
He turns up the roadway to check for their carriage,
pushing against the wind until he finds a break

and stays his horse like a sentry atop the ridge.
The river climbs its banks, tearing planks from the bridge.

VI.

Loose planks bob and disappear downriver. Reins hitched
to the truss, Catherine inches out onto the deck.
The dark water gushes through knotholes in the bridge,

surges over her boots, dashing her face and dress
with mud churned by the current. She pushes her foot
forward, feeling for gaps, shaking—she thinks—like legs

on a wire. Far off, thunder cracks like splitting wood
and she sees the girl fall through fire, the burning tent,
hears the trapped elephant squall like a wailing child.

Then, through the rain, she sees the bent brim of Bob's hat.
He yells *stay where you are* then *take hold of my arm.*
When they clear the bend, the boys rush from the milk shed:

Wallace, stripping wet quilts, hoisting Ted in his arms,
while Lynn runs the team toward the dim light of the barn.

VII.

Lynn leads the horses through the barn's sliding door,
down the lamplit feedway to their stalls. His hair clings
to his forehead and his wet overalls sag, but he moors

them to their stanchions, brushes each down, then cleans
with a hoof-knife the hard clay clotted to their soles.
Wind rattles the bare rafters. On the roof's thin tin

rain hums like a snare. By now, they must be nestled
in dry quilts, warm in the glow of the stove. Their soft
hands must throb, cupping mugs of black tea, but Lynn scales

the ladder into the dark reaches of the loft.
He crawls over damp bales and unbolts the hay door.
Here, above thrashing pines and wind that just won't stop,

he counts breaths between flare and crack, until the storm
moves on, flashing across fields of flax and sweetcorn.

Ashes

Ashfall Fossil Beds near Orchard, Nebraska

The visitor center film calls them
fine-grained pyroclasts, but I remember
more than TV images of clouds.
I still see the human pictures—
the *Geographic* photographer
snapping shots of Saint Helens
until he was covered
and gone—so I call it ash,
because any other name,
though accurate, is not true.

Rain, then wind,
the way it all comes back.
The cottonwood fallen, lodgepole
and white pine lifted wholly
from their roots, and under lightning
my mother, grieving.
By morning the only tree
remaining is fragmented: the ash.

In this spot, before it was
accurately named, the rhinos
lay buried at Ashfall. Ten million years
sealed in sudden dust, each detail
becoming more chilling,
making the story a little truer.
They find grass seeds in teeth,
babies still nursing, frozen
without warning, candid
as photographs.

And sometimes I remember morning
that way, in stills. Not

27

whole movements of time,
but voices behind snapshots,
limousines, faces, but mostly
the words of my mother
becoming true.

The guide says the eruption that
covered these rhinos must have been
a hundred times the blast
Mount Saint Helens let loose.
Imagine dust, he says,
thick as clouds, suddenly choking.

Ashen is what I remember mother saying,
her tears in my mind's photograph
making it impossible to see exactly
what is accurate—but I remember
her saying, No, it's not the way
to remember him. He's so still
and, I remember her saying, ashen.

None of this may be accurate,
the guide might have said more
than a hundred times
Mount Saint Helens, or less.
He might have said Vesuvius,
but Vesuvius is unimagineable,
so I remember Saint Helens,
and maybe it was the words of the minister,
those I never heard, the ashes to ashes
I so desperately needed that I remember
now in the mouth of my mother.

Maybe, after all, it's only
a flashbulb making me

recall these things this way:
a morning so otherwise like another,
words too perfectly
what I'm needing to remember—
her looking out over fallen trees,
saying, this is all that remains,
all there is, truly now, is this ash.

Night Train

Theodore Thompson Genoways, December 28, 1916

He stirs before dawn, tucks a lantern in his pack,
and leans out into the cold. Half-dark, chimney smoke
feathers and molts, circling the frozen window glass,

fading across drifted fields. He wades through snowbanks,
windblown to the eaves of an abandoned milk shed,
and across the barnyard, where leaf-bare cottonwoods

and evergreens stretch from the farm to deeper woods.
His skates curl like a promise in his canvas pack.
At the river's edge, he builds a small fire and sheds

his overshoes, while gusts send a thick rope of smoke
and cherry sparks, swirling toward the distant bank.
Late last August, he honed his father's reading glass

on a knot of bluestem and dried cobs, till the glass
shimmered, grass curled and burned. He piled on scrubwood,
then whole logs. Together, the boys walked the ditch bank,

touching torches to each row, but Ted trailed the pack,
blinking as his brothers—one by one—passed into smoke.
He kindles his lantern. The little light it sheds

casts his legs in wide shadow, down the watershed
and across the river, stretched below like frosted glass.
He buckles his skates, watching the gray thread of smoke

from his chimney stitch across the sheltering woods,
firs straight and green as soldiers. He shoulders his pack
and takes a long, gliding step from the near bank,

buoyed on a scalpel blade of steel, toward the bank
on the far shore. For a moment, the valley—washed
in moonlight, the sky-blue glow of ice and snowpack—

speeds and scrolls by him, as if passing through the glass
of a Pullman car. Boys fresh from the backwoods
crowded the platform that summer morning, coal smoke

dotting girls' dresses with soot as the train left, smoke
clinging to their tear-streaked cheeks. He curls on the bank
under the bridge, waiting for thunder from the woods

to jar ashes, bitternut, bur-oak till they shed
their brittle leaves. Its hiss echoes like breaking glass
or a snake in tall reeds. He braces for impact.

From the bone-black woods, the night train rockets past, packed
with sleeping recruits. It banks through the plume of smoke
it sheds like a skin and slithers on tracks of glass.

Bullroarer

for Gerald Stern

My memory is vague, but goes like this:
Grandpa standing on the lawn
at the old house, showing me a woodblock
painted with storm clouds, lightning, and rain,
in his other hand a leather thong
tied to the block, and at the right time
he begins, wood circling his head,
leather slicing the silence
until the sound unleashed, I swear,
is a rainstorm. *Bullroarer*, he says
as if passing to me a sacred name.

Over dinner it comes up:
he worked in the slaughterhouses in Omaha.
He was only halfway through high school then,
but when the Depression hit,
his brother moved and he found work
where he could find it. He said
he had nightmares at first, the sound of boxcars
moving through cattleyards
crashing together in sequence, from the distance
becoming thunder approaching.
Something in that sound
smacked of blood, carried a memory
white-eyed and bawling.

He went west: worked mostly dirt
out where the only sounds were silence
and storm, each far on the horizon.
Storm tightens a farmer's heart, he said.
The way lightning makes wind crazy,
growing thick and sweet, the aroma of storm,

cattle locked in their pens
baying all night, panicked and slobbering,
clattering horn against horn. *They could shake
the whole fence,* he said, rattle split-posts
like wheels buckling railroad ties.

Grandpa showed me the bullroarer
only once and gave it to me,
never spoke its name again,
something, he said, to keep.
And in keeping I find significance
each night circling the tracks outside my window,
the same engine inside that bullroarer
static, yet spinning, something
that refuses words, something singing
with the energy of motion. Call it train,
call it thunder, but there is something
white-eyed and bawling that stares and storms
generation into generation, something
demanding a sacred name, something
spinning of its own determinate will:
call it wind, call it breath.

III

Into the Storm

He swam the seas before the continents broke water . . .
　　　　　　　　　　　　　—*Moby-Dick*

Cherry-flame sunrise, and already
I'm combing each horizon for signs
of summer squall. Interstate 8 moves on, pulling me
west from Casa Grande, into wind, away
from dawn. If there were luck for me,
lurking here between paloverde and greasewood,
I would see the ancient barkentine
rise triple-mast from the desert floor,
then tack, unmoored, breasting back
to the harbor, a full fathom over waves off Cortéz.
But the world, being what it is,
produces no oceans from sand, its only miracle
a beacon-light stripe through blacktop,
this map, precise to the X of wherever-you-are.

Someday, I want to rent a Volkswagen
in Sonoyta, south of the border, and drive
to the bay of St. George. I've heard real boats sail
places offshore even Spaniards
never whaled. A decade before I read
Moby-Dick, before I linked Old Spice
with ambergris sliced from their bellies,
my grandmother, Avon lady, gave me a plastic whale,
hollowed to hold cologne, aftershave,
and soap, etched with the Cutty Sark. In school, I learned
perfume is acid first, loosed
by bowels to eat beaks of giant squids.
It turns grisly sweet in open air.
That smell is half

of what I remember, the cloud around her,
rousing me from sleep. Oregon,
and because she was older,
mom and dad let my sister work the shore
where a pod of whales beached and spoiled.
I was too young to drag dulled blades
to biologists carving layer
by layer, in hope of finding the riddle's
core. When she slipped,
past midnight, through the camper door,
mom hustled her from her clothes.
She swayed, floating through darkness
toward the bunk, lifting sheets like a jib, enough
to set me adrift.

Who wouldn't believe
a buoyant white hulk, droning its liquid song,
might still roam these skies? Or a ship
might bob on waves rippling
from empty arroyos? Aboard, sailors scrimshaw teeth,
carve ghost whales prowing through hulls
of ocotillo, dry saguaro. They drift
toward distant sierras to drop anchor, strip blubber,
and crack the skull. When the first raindrop comes,
what flowers will burn like tallow
scraped from the inner ear. The wick
wobbles and licks black smoke
into the night sky, forecasting morning, red
as an albino eye. Sailor, take warning.

The One Day

for Donald Hall

The one day no one is watching, everything
will change. Will you notice the birds
chirping backwards? Will the sudden silence
high in the cottonwoods give you windless pause?
When you pass the hitchhiker that one day
will you see yourself this time, seeing it all
from his point of view, trying to get somewhere—
being passed by another truck? This time
will you have that strange impulse to give him
a thumbs up, as if he is offering a signal?
Turn off the road to where gravel might
shake something loose. It's time you slept.

That one day nothing will set the world so right
as rising predawn, checking a trotline by flashlight,
cleaning what you will fry later and eat.
The one day that everything changes, be awake:
feeding will have meaning. Not the cows
come in to eat, not the promise that next time
you will brand, not the brand. It's not even
the feeding, not even the feed. Listen
and look—have you noticed the struggle
of moo? The uncontrolled intake after every
call. Not the moo, but the stirring between.
At sunset, when cattle come to feed in silhouette,

notice how mouths open, how saliva runs in streamers.
It could be silk so light on the wind—slobber, *drool*.
The one day it matters, twisting swirls of slime
will lift like smoke circling from the fire,
before the fire is lit. If you are asleep, you will miss it.
Rise early today. Bow your head. Fry the crappie

and the catfish, but forgo all tartar, all Tabasco.
Taste fish, taste meat. Remember the muscled struggle
that two hours ago was fish. Remember
your one day comes. Remember we put to the ground
what remains of cattle after slaughter; it feeds the grass.
Remember the entrails of fish attract more fish.

Blaze

The earth is peppered with holsteins.
Coals in their eyes clutch the last glimmer
of fire. Rising out of mesquite and clods,
smeared with mud, they answer our calls,
moaning one long vowel,
that tongue-drunk song they know.

We bang a bucket and honk the horn.
Each cow groans a drawled response
but, if we step too close, ducks and stumbles.
This is the moment everything happens,
the deep sigh we take, spotting the last cow,
before closing the gate and counting heads.

They sense it. We are here to brand.
These are not my cows.
When spring comes and trucks to load them,
I will be gone. The work of slaughter
belongs to others I'll never meet.
We do our part, each one. We light the fire.

We lift the calf. We know hotter
means less pain, and we hold the head away
so they don't twist or kick.
But this heifer struggles. Not knowing the blood
ahead, she cries out anyway.
The gloves covering her eyes are cut from leather.

The Killing Floor

. . . and so out of each pen there rolled a steady stream of carcasses,
which the men on the killing-floor had to get out of the way.
                                   —Upton Sinclair, *The Jungle*

I. THE DROVER

> *Theodore Thompson Genoways, Omaha Union Stockyards,*
> *after sundown, November 11, 1932*

Snow furls through the floodlights' potassium flicker,
rides the wash of cattle cars, as they pitch and boom
past the switch to the yards. He squats in a slicker

and hip boots by a fire licking from an oil drum.
After the engineer sounds *all clear,* boys scramble
down rail ties, hooking then rolling back the side doors,

snug against their ramps, yelling and clanging handbells.
When the Burlington westbound clacks the trestleworks—
tracks buckling, rumbling timbers—the drover lowers

his head, then lifts the prod from the coals, smoke billow
trailing to where he pulls the gate open. Cow hooves, worn
smooth, slip on the chute's wet grate. They trip and roll

or slide on their fore-knees. Crowded pinbone to horn,
they shoulder through doors, sprawl like newborns in the mud.
High over the yard, sleepless in his cot, Ted starts

when his brother, the drover, shouts. Flailing, hot-prod
charring their sides, cattle kick till they jump, then trot
on hobbled legs into the maze of the feedlots.

II. MOONSHINING

The boardinghouse roof, past midnight, November 12, 1932

All October, Johannsen slipped cobs of white corn
in the pockets of his smock, to fill two tow sacks
stashed under his bunk. At night, fresh from the kill-floor,

he dipped his fist in troughs or picked the fodder box
of a hog pen for ears, then—while playing poker—
he cupped his mortar and pestle like a soup bowl,

grinding kernels to meal. Now he seals the cooker
and stokes the fire. No one talks, waiting till it boils.
Each dawn, Ted watches this man lift an iron maul

and shout. When the steer lurches into the chute, bowed
like a beggar, he strikes so the sledge splits the skull.
They drop and shudder. Whatever breed, bull or cow,

they buckle to their knees and groan. Their red tongues loll
and jerk like dogs in summer, neck muscles knotted
and twitching. Johannsen smiles when the cooker taps.

The copper coil—packed in a tub of snow—sputters
and drips into the pail. Johannsen dips his cup
under the nipple and takes a long, thoughtful sip.

He settles the mug into Cullen's hand. Blinded
drinking coolant strained through day-old bread, Cullen pulls
a chain all day, sending carcasses down the line

when the cutters call. They wait for his approval—
to take the first drink and grin—before filing by
filling their tins. In a few hours, these same men—tanked

on high shot—will stand side by side on the cut line,
Johannsen swinging the maul, the moon still hanging
full-white and cratered as the face of an angus.

III. THE BIRD-CATCHER
The boardinghouse, daybreak, November 12, 1932

On the docks below Ted's window, stacks of feed hay
rot, riddled with weevils. He watches a fowler,
crouched in rushes by river's edge, hug a ten-gauge,

waiting for mallards to set down. Every hour
since Wallace's boots clambered down the stairs, heavy
as hooves, he has risen again from the same dream

to find the same birder stock-still, but his bevy
grown—a row of headless ducks strung up by their feet
and bleeding out onto the snow and trampled reeds.

He draws the blind. When Wallace returns, wages blown,
drunk and still stinking of blood, Ted must yield the bunk—
its bedsprings spent and sagging with the constant stone

of sleep—to kick the streets till his shift bell is rung.
His eyes comb the yellow stains on his ceiling,
the way a practiced helmsman can sound river depths

or a heron spear a wriggling fish—by reading
ripples for snags or trout. His father always said
Cast toward the center, where bubbles broke and spread

on the dawn-reddened lake, *then watch your cork wobble.*
Wait till it jerks, wait till you see it go under.
The shotgun cracks and repeats, its echoed double

coming like a clear reflection off the water.
Ted peers through a keyhole in the curtains in time
to see: a flock of pintails flap into the air,

the fowler's dog tread against the current, the line
of dockworkers turn from burning wheat and cheer.
And his brother's boots start their slow climb up the stairs.

IV. RENDERING
   Outside the Swift Slaughterhouse, noon, November 12, 1932

Cutters pour from the slaughterhouse doors to the catwalk
above the lot. They lean on the handrail, chewing
crusts smeared with lard, or flop and roll their bloody smocks

into pillows and drowse in the sun. Smoke, spewing
from twin stacks, chokes the yard with the stench of burnt hooves.
Johannsen wets his lips and hands Cullen the flask.

His frosted eyes jitter from the boardinghouse roof
to the tracks below, where a low-riding stake truck
brakes by a frozen calf. Ted squints, his stare fixed

on the workman, untying the tarp of his rig.
When he peels the canvas back, Johannsen elbows
Cullen and says, *Look-it:* dead cows piled three-high, legs

grey and stiff as tipped sawhorses. When early snows
blew in, tracks drifted under dunes, cattle guards sank,
and mavericks wandered the switchyard, snow-blind and lost.

Drovers chained dead calves to the axle by their shanks—
tires chawing mud, gearshift rasping between first
and reverse—until each body would crackle and twist

like an uprooted stump. Now, through the brute silence
blanketing the yard, the workman's hacksaw sings across
the calf's hock like the bow to some grim violin.

He scoops each hoof into a sack and shrouds the carcass
with canvas, to warm in the sun. The shift bell rings
and men shamble through the doors, down the grated stairs,

to the kill-floor. Ted guides Cullen back to his chain
and pulley, watching how his eyes jump when steers
rush the chute. Johannsen yells and swings the hammer.

45

V. HORN

Swift Slaughterhouse, sundown, November 12, 1932

Bone-crush and moan. Over the rattle of hoist chains
lifting gates, Johannsen yells *next!* before the dead bulls
even slump to the shackle trap, the gambrel-man

cuffing each at the hock. The bulls jerk when he pulls
the lever, heaved into the air till the roller
rests in the trolley track. They twist, strung like linen

in a spring breeze, blood and spume drizzling the kill-floor.
One night on the boardinghouse roof, the gambrel-man
whispered, *I seen it, Ted. Knocked a hundred longhorn*

up from Texas—couldn't been more than an hour—
Later, bold on sour mash, Ted asked how. *Strong legs,*
Johannsen slurred, *and split the brow when they lower*

their horns. He straddles the bars of the butcher rig,
clasping the guard with his thighs, while he swings the maul.
Nights like these, when trains idle three-deep in the yards

and drovers desert downed calves, they load every stall
five-full. Even from where Ted stands, scooping innards
and shit with a spade into holes, he hears the thuds,

the clatter of hoof against steel, the moan, the *scream*—
Ted pivots to see Johannsen slumped on the floor,
his purple thigh raveling like frayed hemp, then streams

of blood threading his fingers. Ted hits the buzzer
and runs, dragging Johannsen away from the pen
where the staggered steer froths and smashes his horn, hooked

on the bar, till it snaps and bleeds. When the cut-men
hoist him on the litter, Johannsen stutters, *I'm cooked.*
Once he's gone, each strikes the dead bull for fear or luck.

8:15

Union Stockyards, past dawn, November 13, 1932

and he hasn't shown for work yet.
There is fog. There is hot-rail, steam uncurling,
steam twisting from the half-lit

tracks. There is burlap and wood rat,
oil stain and gnaw, dry cough—drizzle turning flurries,
and he hasn't shown for work yet.

Instead there is cornmeal and crotch rot.
There is turbine and piston, a lead pipe he carries,
steam twisting from the half-lit

cattle cars, dripping slats heavy with slobber and shit.
There is dew in the switchgrass; it's nearing 8:30,
and he hasn't shown for work yet.

There is jam-pack—the low, distant smite
of coupling. There are twin engines warming,
steam twisting from them, half-lit,

chasing parallel tracks. Steam spirits from his lips.
Steam twisting from the half-lit
rails. Sheets drawn, footlocker missing,
and he hasn't shown for work yet.

IV

Three Still Lifes, 1949

I.

Certain nights, when the moon is full, after a shift
    late at the mill, Ted turns the truck toward the creek.

Not to check the gauges or open the headgates,
    it's late, and he's come to hear the water bubble

over the slab, to purge the droning of machines.
    He cuts the engine, stares across the shimmering

ditch to where the weeping willow's tangled shadows
    stretch over fields of corn. Sometimes he wonders

what would happen if he hopped the fencewire, walked rows
    until sunrise. Nothing, or nothing that wouldn't

happen when daylight pales the sky to blue: weevils
    and rootworm, more mud to scrape from his boots.

He turns the key, a crooner's low murmuring from
    the radio, headlights hunting their way back home.

II.

Sarah stands at the sink, sheer curtains ruffling
   in the morning breeze. It's not quite dawn, as she whisks

the batter to the rise and fall of his sleeping.
   Two crows peck at the pelt of something tire-flattened

in the road, skunk or cat. Black as her griddle,
   they hop like grease. Five cakes, dollar-sized, one patty

per plate, corn syrup, toast. Soon the sun will be up.
   She sets the coffee to boil, eases the screendoor closed,

slips into the yard where she can hear them cawing
   and flapping. In the root cellar, she picks two jars

of jelly, then pauses for a moment, listens
   to blood thrum in her ears. The cool damp surrounds her.

She hears footsteps shuffle over the bare floorboards,
   husband and son rattling forks, the clatter of birds.

III.

From the frame's cardboard back, another snapshot falls
    on the doilied dresser. Not the picture Hugh knows—

where he rides his father's wide shoulders, alive in
    the grainy flow of that moment—but a flash

when he was still an unanswered question. His father,
    slump-shouldered and shy, stands past reach of this girl.

She was twenty-two then, and her eyes were lighter.
    Every spring, she gathered wildflowers in baskets

for their nightstand and sill above the kitchen sink.
    A breeze moves the curtains. Through the open window

he sees her brushing her hair away from her face,
    a line of white-capped clouds riding the bluff so fast

the room seems to turn. Still-framed, this picture burns
    behind his eyes: sky ocean-wide, her body full sail.

For My Father, Who Does Not Dance

When he was fifteen, he built a telescope
to escape gravity, because small towns
have their own orbits and pull. His,
like Mercury, marked years in circles
shrinking smaller. He felt friction
in stasis, the disembodiment of drift.

Those were nights before new physics
could invent his freedom, before Heisenberg
cast everything into motion and question.
My father knew where he was.
What he couldn't say was velocity
or course, because those were nights

before the earth was set to music,
before rooftops danced with subatomic energy.
He looked skyward for some glimmer,
the chance that every action has an equal
and opposite, that another body, somewhere
in this universe, might feel him spinning.

Landscape with Dust

A roiling billow, filling shadows and shafts
   of light latticed through shelterbelt trees,

ranges over corn rows and wide, dead-eyed cattle,
   a ghostly brown cloud of everywhere I've been.

It was here—Bayard, Nebraska—in this noon-heat
   shimmying off a washboard road, he saved

their town, or so I'm always told. Each day,
   my grandfather turned the crank that brought

water to the valley, an orange flume that fanned
   into every field. I've heard those mud-rusted

threads squawk like an angry crow, heard
   the truck ticking in the sun, while static

cycled on the radio. Whole years pass this way,
   noon seamless into night, cicada-whirr

from the thick vines rising and falling
   like a flooded engine. But now it's a story

too often told to be true, each detail
   familiar as a leather glove that holds

the form of his hand, his fist
   white-knuckled by work, long after it is laid

on the nightstand and the man who shaped it sleeps.
   Another moon climbs in the trees, then rolls

across the blue-lit dark of another night sky.
   Day breaks with me standing in the classroom

where my father learned to write his name,
   floorboards upturned by the trunk of a cottonwood

shouldering through the rafters and shingles
   into the open sky. It seems impossible now,

everything I've been asked to believe,
   and somewhere short miles from here

the name we share disappears from the stone.
   Then, from all stones rowed like teeth,

from this pocked blackboard, the slate
   he toted home. The letters ripple and fade

like mirages crouched at floodpoints in the road.
   We speak, my family, as every family

must, in the scrawl of bloodlines, mute
   tangle-vine willow tracking ancestry to a clan

of strangers. I won't look for him within
   any described plot, barbed wire fencing dead

from the living. Each day the water came,
   diverted by ditchwork, from somewhere

he had never been, but there it was: no miracle,
   no one saved, just water to measure and dole

to farmers who paid. The day he died,
   the water froze in those gutters

but when spring came the ditches ran high
   with snowmelt and every mourner was out

tending his rows. I won't look for him here,
   won't question anymore the silent stone,

tumbledown school, or the house crowded
   now with another family I'll never know.

The script of tire tracks I leave for them in the gravel
    is an heirloom for safekeeping, the cursive

of stones, the little cloud that spreads behind me
    lingering barely a heartbeat in the memory

of the farmer who looks up now to engine-roar
    kicking dust into the stippled mote-light

of the barn where my grandfather one late evening
    doubled and bent to one knee.

Three Sonnets Written in Clouds

I.

Glenshaw, Pennsylvania, 1979

Under another sky, I stumbled over stones.
My sister bowed to scales for the right hand,
falling and rising in the piano teacher's window.
I tromped woods behind the house, unearthing cans,
stooping to eye the globe of a puffball mushroom,
overturning a rock blanketed by maple leaves
and bark peelings. The underside of the stone,
moist and brown with dirt, bore one word: *Baby.*
My throat closed. My head lolled skyward:
Kentucky coffee trees, sycamores. Somewhere
a gray squirrel loosed a nut from a shagbark tree.
I heard it tick from limb to limb, but never
hit the ground. I ran to the house, scared,
sending clouds of ripe spores spiraling.

II.

I go back to that day, making the turn to the lake.
I've watched daily decay in Patton Springs; still,
I won't go to their frontier graves.
The sign whispers *one mile.* I almost ask Bill,
almost say *come with me*, but I have too many jobs
and he came to fish. The sun peels skin
off the lake's face all day. I clear moss from docks,
drag logs of trees I can't name. Cows come in
to wade and stare at that strange apparition,
purling across water, casting flies in fluid S's,
light from his sunglasses like the start of a wish.
It's then I see it: this other man's vision
of death, his best impression of a fly's breath,
real enough to fool one shallow fish.

III.

Scottsbluff, Nebraska, 1986

Under what water or sky could I even begin
to strike open mouth? When I was thirteen,
my mother stuttered like an engine
the same word, *How, How?* Bowed beneath
the hood of a '58 Chevy, her father's heart
went dead. Christened Theodore H. Cox,
grease-script *Harold*s double-stitched his shirts.
They carved *Ted*—in single quotes—in the rock.
We left under threat of rain, thunderheads rolling,
weaving patterns through rows of grain.
I remembered how pain swelled grandmother's knee
when barometer needles sank, trolling
over clouds as if answers were fish or rain.
Skies coil and darken, but lightning never strikes me.

Late Refrains for a Grandfather

Theodore Thompson Genoways, dead January 19, 1980

I.

I can picture him only in the climate of work:
letting a head of water through floodgates or
stacking hay, silent and smooth as the baler's belt.

For years on factory floors, he shoveled beet sugar
into brown-paper bags, or scooped guts slit
from rows of hanging carcasses; this I know,

but nothing else. More and more, I find myself
trying to read the dustings of hay that trail
heavy loads—bales, mowed and rolled, belt-tied

to flatbeds threading these narrow country roads.
More and more, I find myself driving too close
behind, hoping for a face in the side mirror I know.

II.

Would he dismiss all this as foolishness, say
he spent as much time sleeping as at work? Or
is that just the way I remember him, old man

with callused hands and a voice gone trembly,
mumbling, *let grandpa rest his eyes for a minute.* . . .
Now he is tight-lipped. The wide yellow throat

of the meadowlark and wind's hoarse breath
were the only sounds, all summer I spent out west.
Days I walked roads looking for traces of the man,

but found only fallen fencewire, rows to hoe. My cousin
cupped his hand to an irrigation pipe, said *you try,*
but the sucking water choked, like a word in my throat.

III.

States away, twenty years dead, the shift bell
still rings for him. I call dad late at night to ask
what kind of truck he drove, which railroads shook

the stockyards. On scholarship in Texas, I took
weekend work on a ranch, a know-nothing egghead
locals grinned at. What they didn't know was

I wasn't there for five bucks an hour, for bruises
or backaches. I wasn't there to castrate
or brand. When hollow half oil drums shook

with range feed, I felt something pounding in me;
the moan of the central pivot turning in wheat fields
was the language I needed to say who he was.

IV.

Ted Genoways. Same as me. Gone before I had
turned eight. Dad stroked my hair to rouse me
and led me across the hall, where my sister sat

with my mother, blinking away sleep. When dad
choked on the words, I cried, not knowing
why. I've heard they tie the thumbs of the dead

to hold their arms crossed, use spray paint or rouge
to brighten their cheeks, sew their lips with invisible
thread. That snowy morning, new year, we sat

in hard pews. Around me, whispers rehearsed
lies for the reception: *passed away, departed soul,
met his reward,* when they really meant *stone dead.*

V.

What they couldn't afford, he built out of oak:
pull cars and soldiers for dad, square tables
with drop leaves, a chest of drawers, cupboards until

the rooms were filled. When grandma moved,
after fifteen years without him, we had to choose
what to keep, what to split and crush to fit

in the dirt-alley dumpster. We stood bookshelves
back to back and shook our heads: one thirty-four
inches wide, another thirty-six. Not until

I took down books—gunfighter memoirs, *Book
of Indian-Crafts*—did I realize that thirty years in a house
they finally owned, he had cut every board to fit.

VI.

The hour of his death, he was stacking cinder blocks.
Out there in the near dusk, the heat in his chest—
like an August noon-sun—must have shocked him.

The doctor gave him Tums, but on the drive back
from Scottsbluff, pain stretched down his arm like
the broken yellow line limping to the house where he lived

and died. My mother said, *no,* I couldn't see him
like this, the dim-eyed undertaker's botched work.
I stayed in the pew, but over the vamping hymn

everyone said, *threads, you can see the threads
stitching his lips.* The summer before we married,
I took my wife to see that place where no one living lives.

VII.

When the house at last stood an empty shell,
grandma brought from the broom closet
a case full of old tapes, arranged by name

and dates like rows of tombstones. In his old age,
he took his recorder to the senior home, asked
pioneers and war vets to retell their lives.

And last here among them, a tape with my name.
The house stands there still, gutted for remodeling,
but the walls echo as he begins again: *My name*

is Ted Genoways, and in this recording on this
the ninth day of March, 1978, I'm going to relate
some of my life—

The Dead Have a Way of Returning

the way an echo returns:
only partly.
In this way, he left himself
in corners, between the pages of books,
his thin frame slipping through windows
cracked open, becoming in place of himself

his shadow, the way a word
whispered in darkness
seems without source or direction,
disappearing so completely in silence
he wondered
was it a word?

or something deeper?—
something like feeling the earth shift
not in tremor, but the slow movement
of drift. In the way of geology films
speeding the action forward
so eons pass in seconds,

so he imagined himself
sliding into this darkness,
both past and also present,
into the chance that he might touch
the echo
and vanish, yet

he becomes a hundred children.

A NOTE ON THE AUTHOR

Ted Genoways was educated at Nebraska Wesleyan University (B.A.), Texas Tech University (M.A.), and the University of Virginia (M.F.A.). He is the editor of *The Selected Poems of Miguel Hernández* (2001) and author of three chapbooks, most recently, *Anna, washing*. His poems have appeared in *DoubleTake, New England Review, New Republic, Ploughshares, Shenandoah, Virginia Quarterly Review*, and twice received the Guy Owen Poetry Prize from *Southern Poetry Review*. The founding editor of the literary journal *Meridian*, he now lives in Minneapolis, where he is an editor at the Minnesota Historical Society Press.

A NOTE ON THE PRIZE

The Samuel French Morse Poetry Prize was established in 1983 by the Northeastern University Department of English in order to honor Professor Morse's distinguished career as teacher, scholar, and poet. The members of the prize committee are Francis C. Blessington, Joseph deRoche, Victor Howes, Ruth Lepson, Stuart Peterfreund, Guy Rotella, and Ellen Scharfenberg.